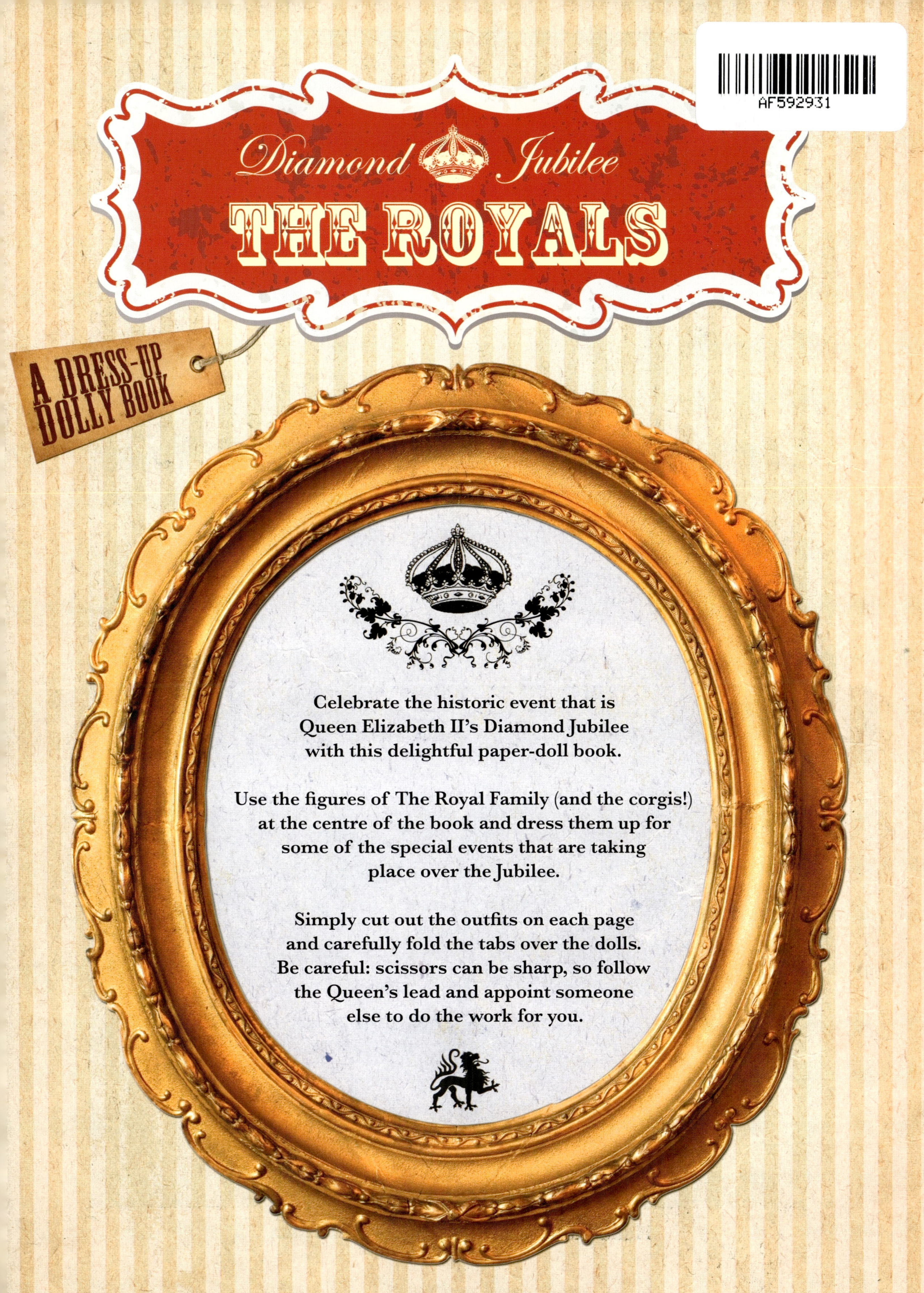

Celebrate the historic event that is Queen Elizabeth II's Diamond Jubilee with this delightful paper-doll book.

Use the figures of The Royal Family (and the corgis!) at the centre of the book and dress them up for some of the special events that are taking place over the Jubilee.

Simply cut out the outfits on each page and carefully fold the tabs over the dolls. Be careful: scissors can be sharp, so follow the Queen's lead and appoint someone else to do the work for you.

GOD SAVE THE QUEEN

HM (Her Majesty) Queen Elizabeth II celebrates 60 years on the throne over the weekend of 2–5 June 2012. The only other British monarch to celebrate a Diamond Jubilee was Queen Victoria in 1897. Queen Elizabeth II came to the throne on 6 February 1952, and her coronation, which took place on 2 June 1953, was watched on TV by millions of people. The Queen's coronation was the first ever to be televised and was also the world's first major international event to be broadcast on TV.

Elizabeth married Philip – a prince of Greek and Danish heritage – in 1947, and they have four children: Charles, Anne, Andrew and Edward. Philip was given the title Duke of Edinburgh shortly before his marriage to Elizabeth, and he also holds honorary appointments and ranks in the Armed Services.

Queen Elizabeth II is known for her handbags and hats, and has donned 5,000 of the latter during her reign. And as for what the Queen carries in her handbag, *Majesty* magazine reports that it holds a comb, a handkerchief, a small gold compact and a tube of lipstick. On Sundays, the Queen carries paper money to place in the collection plate at church.

Cut a slit along the red line and slot the dolly's head through the gap.

HEIR APPARENT

Charles is the eldest son of Queen Elizabeth II and Prince Philip. He automatically became Heir Apparent and Duke of Cornwall when Elizabeth ascended to the throne. He was created Prince of Wales in 1958, becoming the first Prince of Wales since 1936. He also holds the titles of Earl of Chester, Duke of Rothesay, Earl of Carrick and Baron Renfrew, Lord of the Isles and Prince and Great Steward of Scotland.

The Prince of Wales married Camilla Parker Bowles on 9 April 2005. After the wedding, Camilla became known as HRH (Her Royal Highness) The Duchess of Cornwall. When The Prince of Wales accedes to the throne, she will be known as HRH The Princess Consort.

The Prince of Wales currently holds the ranks of Admiral in the Royal Navy, Air Chief Marshal in the Royal Air Force and General in the Army, and often wears one of his military uniforms to royal and formal functions.

Camilla's favourite designer is Anna Valentine, whose dresses she wore to both her own wedding to Charles, and to Kate and Will's. She often wears hats designed by Philip Treacy.

Diamond Jubilee
WILLIAM & KATE
THE NEWLYWEDS
Cut out this stand, fold back along the dotted lines and display next to your dollies!

THE NEWLYWEDS

HRH (His Royal Highness) Prince William of Wales and Miss Catherine Middleton married on 29 April 2011, so depending on whose definition you follow, they may still be considered newlyweds.

Prince William is the elder son of the Prince of Wales and the late Diana, Princess of Wales. Following his marriage to Kate, the title The Duke of Cambridge was conferred on him by his grandmother (the Queen), and Kate therefore became The Duchess of Cambridge.

The couple has made their home in Anglesey, Wales, where William is stationed as a fully operational Search and Rescue Pilot with the Royal Air Force. He is also still a Lieutenant in the Household Cavalry.

Kate is a big fan of Issa, and she has worn dresses by the designer on many occasions, including the famous blue dress she wore to the couple's engagement announcement. However, Kate's wedding dress was designed by Sarah Burton of Alexander McQueen. Although Kate has designer taste, she's also famed for rocking high street fashion like Reiss.

Diamond Jubilee
HARRY
&
THE CORGIS
CUTE AND CUDDLY
ROYALS
Cut out this stand,
fold back along
the dotted lines
and display next
to your dollies!

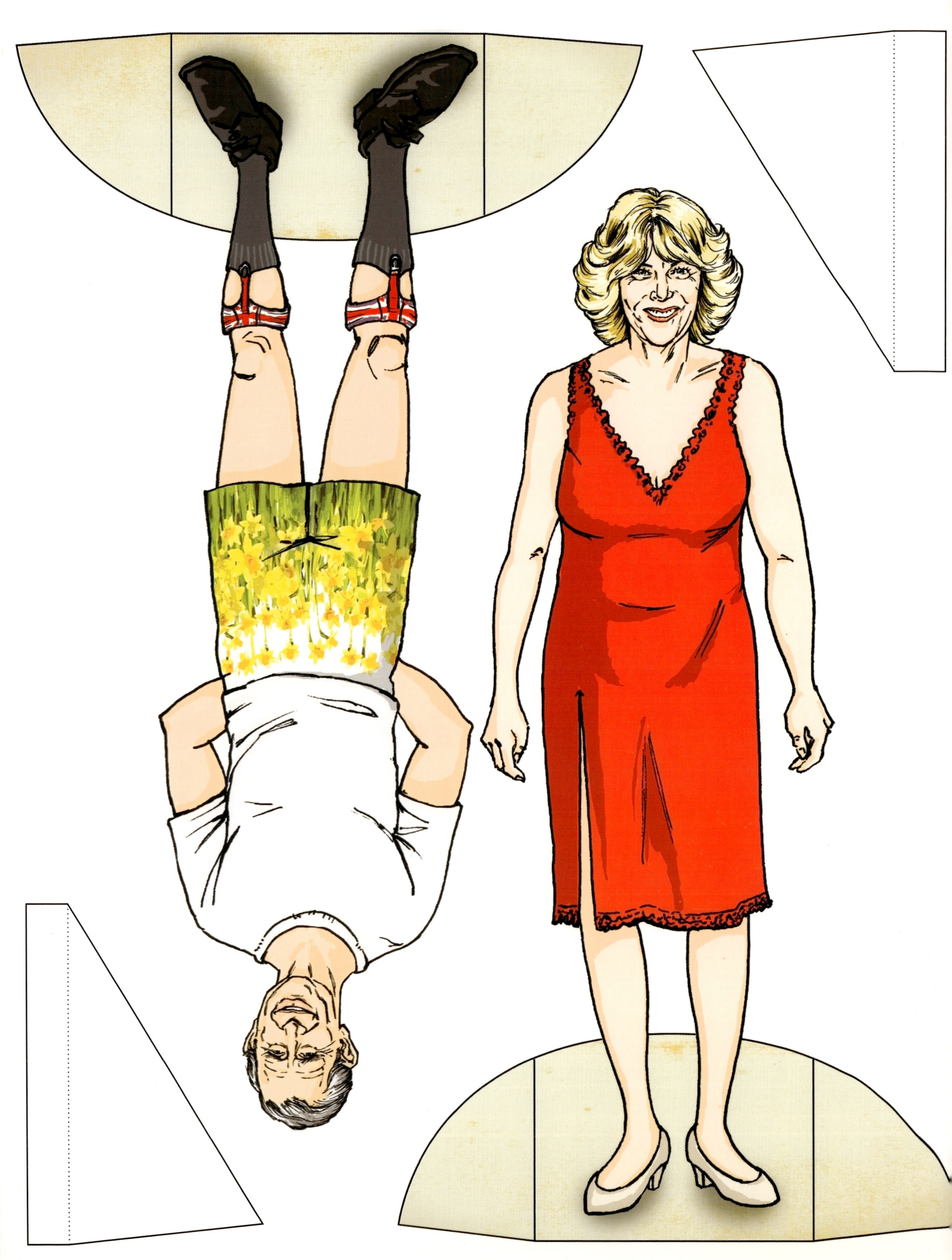

D of E

THE CUTE AND CUDDLY ROYALS

Prince Henry (always known as Prince Harry) is the younger son of the Prince of Wales and the late Diana, the Princess of Wales. On his 18th birthday, the Queen gave Harry his own unique coat of arms.

In May 2005, Prince Harry entered Royal Military Academy Sandhurst to begin his training as an officer in the British Army. Prince Harry joined the Household Cavalry, and served in Afghanistan for more than two months from the end of 2007 to early 2008. He is now training to be a helicopter pilot with the Army Air Corps.

Over the years, The Royal Family have had scores of dogs as their family pets – from pugs to greyhounds, King Charles Spaniels to corgis. The Queen favours corgis, and at present she owns four: Linnet, Monty, Willo and Holly.

The corgis travel with the Queen to the various royal residences, and despite her busy schedule she looks after them herself as much as possible. It's said that the Queen always keeps a stash of chocolate drops in her handbag exclusively for them.

Diamond Jubilee
ELIZABETH
&
PHILLIP
GOD SAVE THE QUEEN
Cut out this stand, fold back along the dotted lines and display next to your dollies!
Queenie

ANYONE FOR TEA?

With tea, cakes and a beautiful garden to stroll through, the garden parties at Buckingham Palace are among the most relaxed and informal royal events. The Queen hosts at least three at Buckingham Palace every year, and around 8,000 guests attend each. From all walks of life, they have been invited on the recommendation of organisations such as the Civil Service, the Armed Forces, the Diplomatic Corps and charities.

The parties take place between 4.00 p.m. and 6.00 p.m, and around 27,000 cups of tea, 20,000 sandwiches (crusts removed) and 20,000 slices of cake are served from a 125-metre-long buffet, with 400 waiting staff on duty. The Queen and The Duke of Edinburgh, accompanied by other members of The Royal Family, circulate among the guests after the National Anthem has been played. Although the garden parties are relaxed events, most people like to dress up for their special day, and the Queen and Prince Philip always look smart for the occasion. Perhaps when the tea is drunk and the guests have departed, however, the pair like to kick back, relax and watch a little TV.

Diamond Jubilee
CHARLES & CAMILLA
HEIR APPARENT
Cut out this stand, fold back along the dotted lines and display next to your dollies!
C&C
C&C

DOWN ON THE FARM

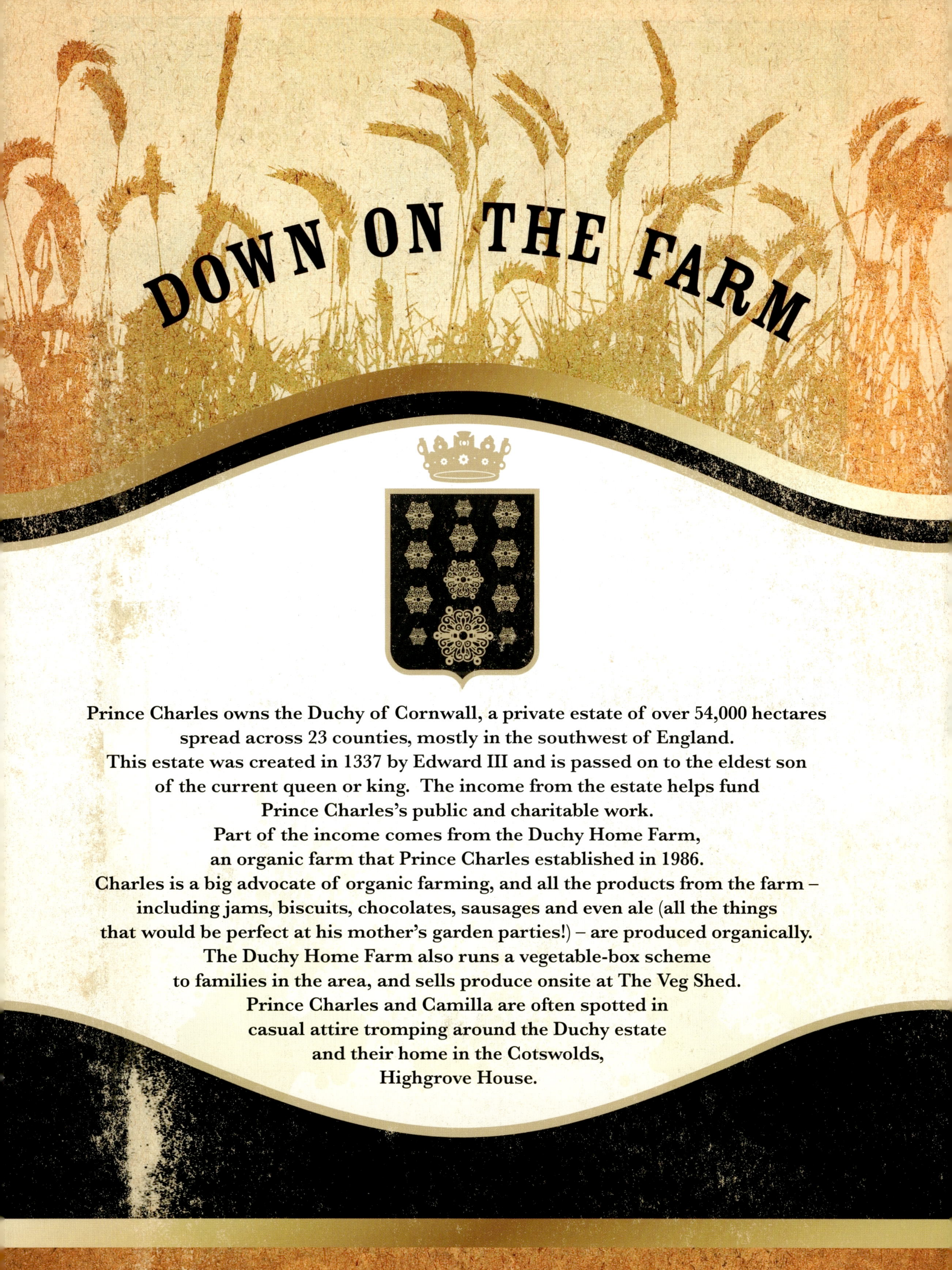

Prince Charles owns the Duchy of Cornwall, a private estate of over 54,000 hectares spread across 23 counties, mostly in the southwest of England. This estate was created in 1337 by Edward III and is passed on to the eldest son of the current queen or king. The income from the estate helps fund Prince Charles's public and charitable work. Part of the income comes from the Duchy Home Farm, an organic farm that Prince Charles established in 1986. Charles is a big advocate of organic farming, and all the products from the farm – including jams, biscuits, chocolates, sausages and even ale (all the things that would be perfect at his mother's garden parties!) – are produced organically. The Duchy Home Farm also runs a vegetable-box scheme to families in the area, and sells produce onsite at The Veg Shed. Prince Charles and Camilla are often spotted in casual attire tromping around the Duchy estate and their home in the Cotswolds, Highgrove House.

Cut a slit along the red line and slot the dolly's head through the gap.

ROYAL RODEO

The Duke and Duchess of Cambridge took their first official trip as a married couple to Canada in the summer of 2011. It was Kate's first trip to North America, and she and her husband were a royal hit with the crowds. Prince William and his bride launched the Calgary Stampede, an annual rodeo, exhibition and festival event. The couple was suitably decked out in casual cowboy gear – both of them in white 10-gallon Smithbilt cowboy hats, cowboy boots and jeans. The Prince sported a plaid shirt and Kate wore a lovely Alice Temperley blouse.

DRESSING DOWN

Prince Harry has decided to pursue a military career. He holds the rank of Captain in the Army and was awarded an Apache Flying Badge in 2011. Harry has already served in Afghanistan, and it is expected that he may return for another tour in the near future. Prince Harry works hard, but he also plays hard: he's a fan of polo, rugby, motocross and skiing – and the famous London night club, Raffles.

The corgis accompany the Queen to her residences, and perhaps when they are away from Buckingham Palace and the London paparazzi they are allowed to have Dress-down Fridays and break out their casual gear.

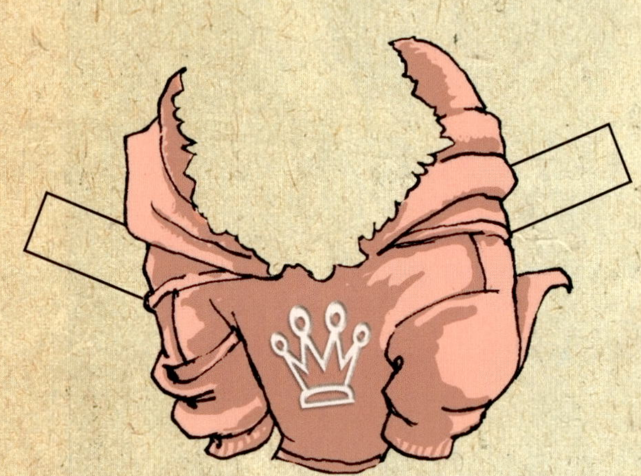

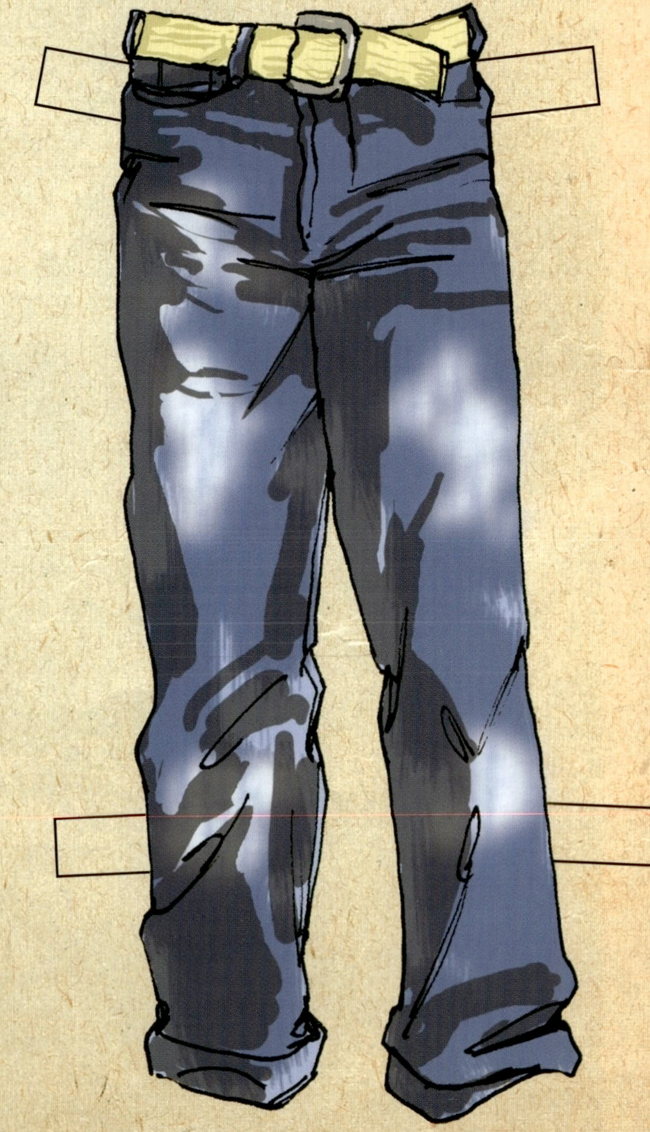

SUNBIRD
PENGUIN

Published by Ladybird Books Ltd 2012
A Penguin Company
Penguin Books Ltd, 80 Strand, London, WC2R 0RL, UK
Penguin Books Australia Ltd, Camberwell, Victoria, Australia
Penguin Group (NZ), 67 Apollo Drive, Rosedale, Auckland
0632, New Zealand (a division of Pearson New Zealand Ltd)

Sunbird is a trade mark of Ladybird Books Ltd

Illustrations by duncansmithstudio.com

www.ladybird.com

ISBN: 978-1-40939-110-4

002 - 10 9 8 7 6 5 4 3 2
Printed in China